Solve all your Maths problems with CGP!

This fantastic CGP book is the best way to help pupils
get to grips with Year 2 Problem Solving.

It's packed with bite-sized tests that get tougher
as pupils build up their skills. By the end of the book they'll have
practised answering the trickiest of problem-solving questions.

We've even included full answers to every question
— plus a handy chart to check progress too!

What CGP is all about

Our sole aim here at CGP is to produce the highest quality books
— carefully written, immaculately presented and
dangerously close to being funny.

Then we work our socks off to get them out to you
— at the cheapest possible prices.

Published by CGP

Editors: Liam Dyer, Samuel Mann, Caroline Purvis and Caley Simpson

With thanks to Sarah George and Gail Renaud for the proofreading.

With thanks to Jan Greenway for the copyright research.

ISBN: 978 1 78908 636 2

1 pence coin © iStock.com/coopder1
2 pence coin © iStock.com/peterspiro
10 pence coin © iStock.com/john shepherd
20 pence coin © iStock.com/Jaap2
50 pence coin © iStock.com/duncan1890
Graphics used throughout the book © www.edu-clips.com
Printed by Elanders Ltd, Newcastle upon Tyne.

Based on the classic CGP style created by Richard Parsons.

Text, design, layout and original illustrations © Coordination Group Publications Ltd. (CGP) 2020
All rights reserved.

Photocopying this book is not permitted, even if you have a CLA licence.
Extra copies are available from CGP with next day delivery • 0800 1712 712 • www.cgpbooks.co.uk

Contents

Test 1 2

Test 2 4

Test 3 6

Test 4 8

Test 5 10

Test 6 12

Test 7 14

Test 8 16

Test 9 18

Test 10 20

Test 11 22

Test 12 24

Answers 26

Progress Chart 30

How to Use this Book

- This book contains 12 tests, all geared towards improving your problem solving skills.

- Each test is out of 8 marks and should take about 10 minutes to complete.

- Each test starts with some warm-up questions.

- The tests increase in difficulty as you go through the book.

- Answers and a Progress Chart can be found at the back of the book.

Test 1

Warm up

1. Count on in steps of 2.

   6, 8, ..., ..., ..., ...

   1 mark

2. Use the number cards on the right to make... | 1 | 2 | 5 | 8 |

   a) ... the biggest possible 2-digit number.

   .... 1 mark

   b) ... the smallest possible 2-digit number.

   .... 1 mark

3. Draw a circle around half of the balloons.

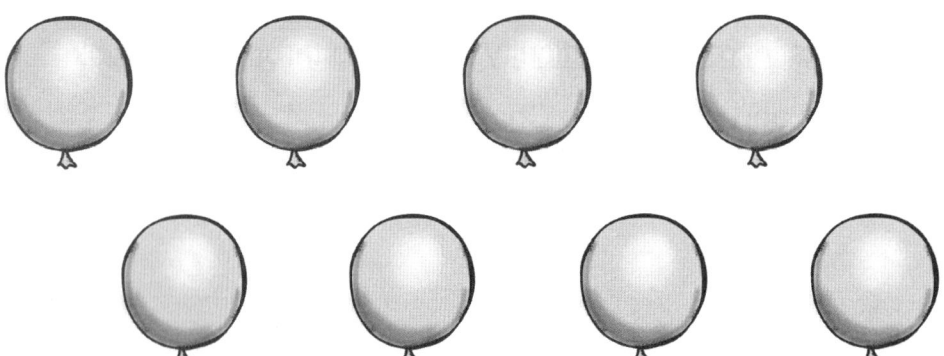

1 mark

4. Kemal, Lydia and Amy are comparing their heights.

Kemal   Lydia   Amy

Who is the tallest?

.... 1 mark

Who is the shortest?

.... 1 mark

5. Write two different sums that have the answer 8.

Use a different pair of numbers for each sum.

.... + ... = 8   .... + ... = 8

2 marks

END OF TEST

/ 8

Test 2

Warm up

1. Use the numbers shown to write two correct subtractions.

   | 5 | 7 | 9 |

   .... − .... = 2   .... − .... = 2

   2 marks

2. What number is three more than seventeen?

   ....

   1 mark

3. Isabel wants to buy a bike that is lighter than 10 kg.

   Draw a ring around the bike she should buy.

   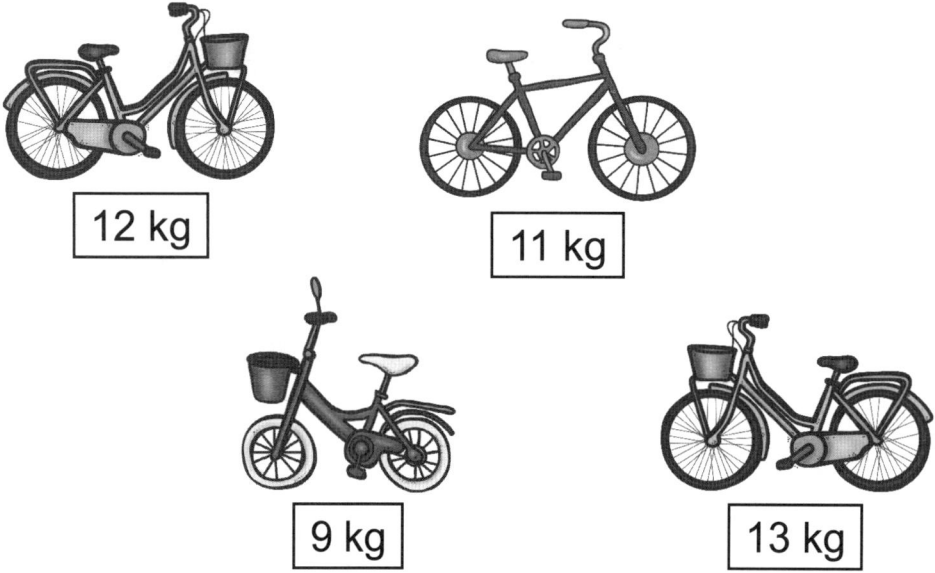

   12 kg   11 kg

   9 kg   13 kg

   1 mark

4. Draw lines to match each shape to its name.

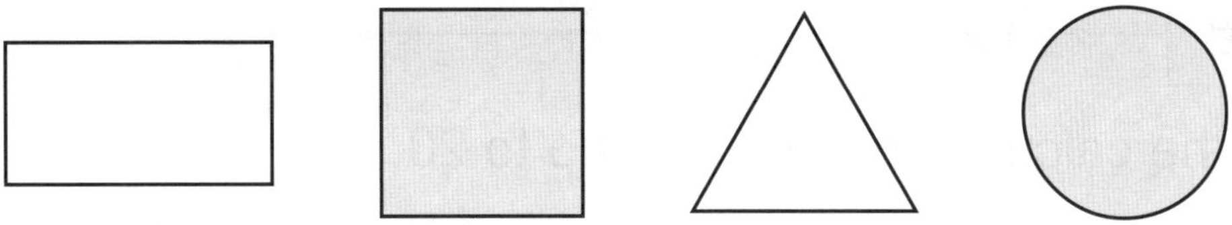

Triangle   Rectangle   Circle   Square

2 marks

5. Ezra has these coins in his pocket.

Which coin is worth the most? Write down its value.

....
1 mark

Which coin is worth more than 5p
but less than 20p? Write down its value.

....
1 mark

END OF TEST

/ 8

Test 3

Warm up

1. Circle the calculations that add up to 20.

    16 + 5   11 + 9   12 + 7   14 + 6

    2 marks

2. If today is Thursday....

    a) ... what day was it the day before yesterday?

    .... *1 mark*

    b) ... what day is it the day after tomorrow?

    .... *1 mark*

3. Put a tick in the box below the shape that has exactly one quarter shaded.

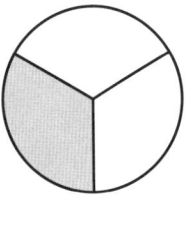 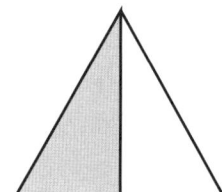 

☐   ☐   ☐

1 mark

4. Three children run one lap of a field. Their times are shown below.

   Jason: 2 minutes and 38 seconds

   Harvey: 3 minutes and 4 seconds

   Thea: 2 minutes and 56 seconds

   Who was quicker than Thea?

   ....

   1 mark

5. There are three bananas in a bunch.

   How many bananas are there in two bunches?

   .... bananas

   1 mark

   How many bananas are there in four bunches?

   .... bananas

   1 mark

   END OF TEST

   / 8

Test 4

Warm up

1. List all the odd numbers that are less than 10.

   ....

   1 mark

2. Draw dots to complete each number sentence.

   a)  + 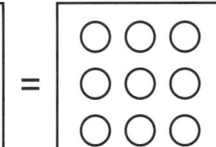 =

   b) 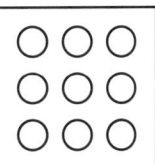 −  =

   2 marks

3. Draw lines from each jug to the right description.

   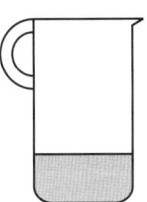   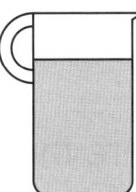   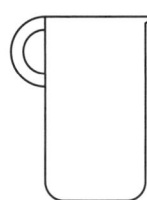

   empty   less than half full   half full   more than half full

   2 marks

4. Look at the pictures below.

   How many cuboids are there?

   .... cuboids

   1 mark

5. Dana draws shapes to show the number 28.
   Each shape represents a ten or a one.

   Ben's number is **3 more** than Dana's number.

   Draw the fewest number of shapes
   that can be used to show Ben's number.

   2 marks

   END OF TEST

   / 8

Test 5

Warm up

1. Fill in the missing numbers.

   ☐ —one less→ ☐ —five more→ 9

   2 marks

2. Circle the correct calculation.

   5 + 10 = 20   15 − 5 = 20   20 − 5 = 15

   1 mark

3. Ava is facing the tree. She makes a clockwise turn to face the squirrel.

   Circle the turn she makes.

   a three-quarter turn clockwise   a quarter turn clockwise   a half turn clockwise

   1 mark

   She makes another turn in the **same direction** until she is facing the tree again.

   Describe the turn she makes.

   Ava makes a ....

   ....

   1 mark

4. Amed does the calculation 4 × 5 = 20.

   Tick the addition that gives the same answer.

   4 + 4 + 4 + 4 ☐   4 + 4 + 4 + 4 + 4 + 4 ☐

   5 + 5 + 5 + 5 ☐   5 + 5 + 5 + 5 + 5 ☐

   1 mark

5. Two cats are playing outside.

   5 kg   4 kg

   What is the total mass of the two cats?

   .... kg

   1 mark

   A dog joins the two cats.
   The total mass of **all** the animals is 19 kg.

   What is the mass of the dog?

   .... kg

   1 mark

   END OF TEST

   / 8

Test 6

Warm up

1. Which number...

   a) ... is twice as big as eight? ....

   b) ... is half as big as twenty? ....

   2 marks

2. Circle three numbers that add up to 10.

         1   2   4   5   6   9

   1 mark

3. Look at the shapes below.

   Shape A   **Shape B**

   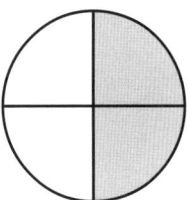 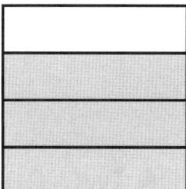

   Circle the correct word in each sentence.

   One (half / quarter) of shape A is shaded.

   Three (halves / quarters) of shape B is shaded.

   1 mark

4. Burt measures the lengths of some bugs.

Worm
9 cm

Spider
5 cm

Slug
11 cm

Write the bugs in order. Start with the shortest.

....

shortest ⎯⎯⎯⎯⎯⎯⎯⎯⎯⎯⎯→ longest

1 mark

Write <, > or = in the box.

length of the worm ☐ length of the slug

1 mark

5. Pinar buys the toys on the right.
   She pays with a £10 note.

   £2   £5

   How much change does she get?

   £................

   2 marks

END OF TEST

/ 8

Test 7

Warm up

1. Circle the calculation that gives the bigger answer.

   a) 3 × 5   or   8 × 2   b) 2 × 10   or   5 × 5

   2 marks

2. Use two of the number cards on the right to make... | 3 | 4 | 7 | 8 |

   a) ... the smallest odd 2-digit number.

   .... _1 mark_

   b) ... the biggest even 2-digit number.

   .... _1 mark_

3. Mia says, "4 + 16 = 20, so 40 + 160 = 200".

   Draw lines to match pairs of numbers that add up to 200.

   Use Mia's number fact to help you.

110		150
130		180
90		50
20		70

   2 marks

4. Put these shapes in order of the number of sides they have. Start with the smallest number of sides.

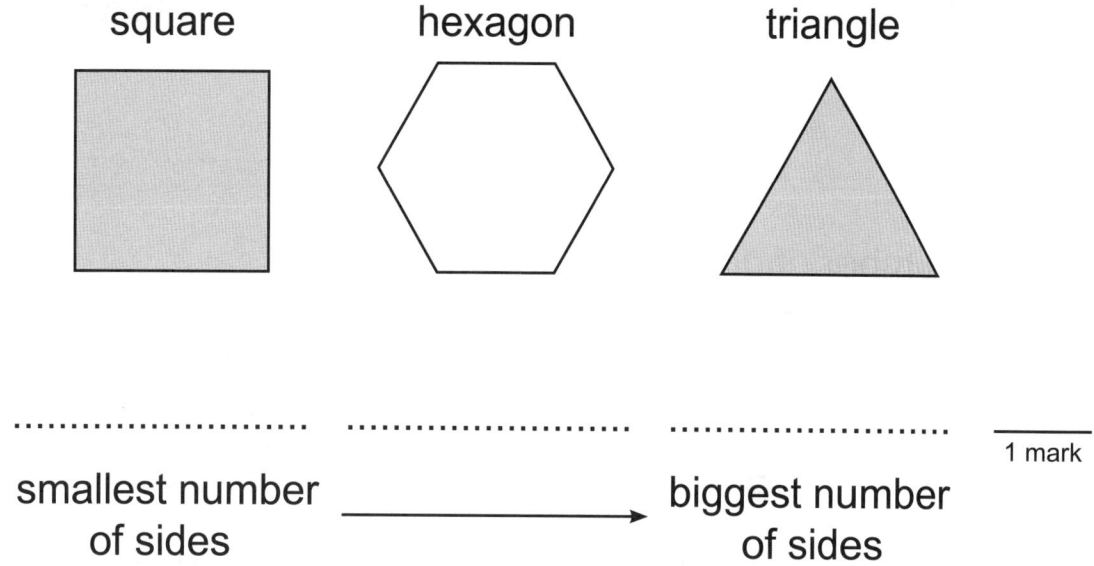

....
1 mark

smallest number of sides ⟶ biggest number of sides

5. Look at the baby crocodile on the scale below.

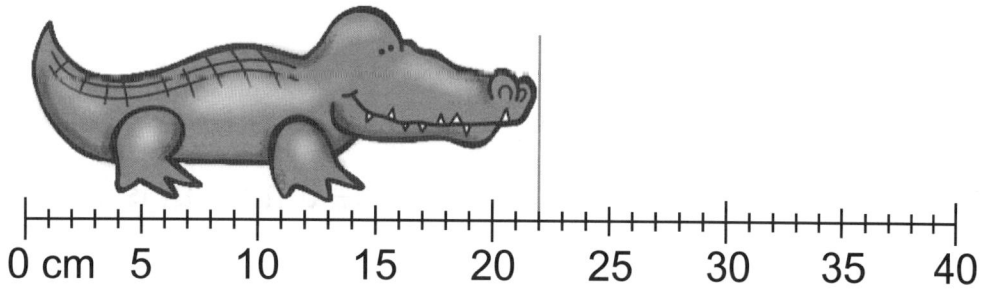

The baby crocodile grows by 16 cm.

How long is it now?

.... cm
1 mark

END OF TEST

/ 8

Test 8

Warm up

1. Work out 3 + 5 + 8.

   .... 1 mark

2. The number of dots in the patterns below increases by 3 each time.

     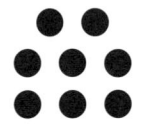 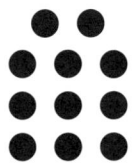

   Pattern 1   Pattern 2   Pattern 3   Pattern 4

   How many dots will there be in...

   a) ... Pattern 5?   b) ... Pattern 7?

   .... 2 marks

3. Draw hands on each clock to show the time that is...

   ... 20 minutes after 10 am.   ... 15 minutes before 3 pm.

   2 marks

4. Look at these 3D shapes.

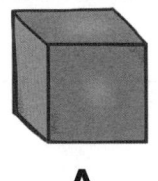 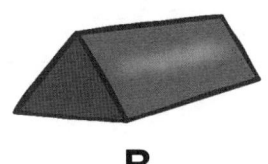 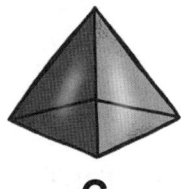

    A   B   C

Which shape has the fewest vertices?

.... 1 mark

Which shape has the most faces?

.... 1 mark

5. The ticket prices for a theme park are shown on the right.

| 1-day ticket | £15 |
| 2-day ticket | £27 |

How much more does a 2-day ticket cost than a 1-day ticket?

£ .... 1 mark

END OF TEST

/ 8

Test 9

Warm up

1. Look at the number 83.
   Write the number that has...

   a) ... one more ten and six more ones.   ....

   b) ... half the number of tens.   ....

   2 marks

2. Circle three numbers that add up to 15.

   2   5   7   8   9

   1 mark

3. What is $\frac{3}{4}$ of 8?

   .... *1 mark*

4. Sara runs for one hour and two minutes.

   How many minutes does she run for?

   .... minutes *1 mark*

5. A large paddling pool costs £40.
A small paddling pool costs £18 **less**.

How much does a small paddling pool cost?

£ ....

1 mark

6. Masood buys ice lollies in packs of 10.
He buys 3 packs.

Josephine buys ice lollies in packs of 5.
She buys 7 packs.

How many more ice lollies does Josephine have than Masood?

.... ice lollies

2 marks

END OF TEST

/ 8

Test 10

Warm up

1. Fill in the missing numbers on this number line.

   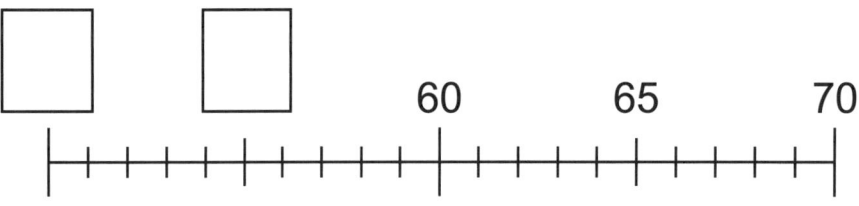

   1 mark

2. Join up the calculations with the same answer.

   20 ÷ 5   8 ÷ 2

   50 ÷ 10   6 ÷ 2

   15 ÷ 5   10 ÷ 2

   2 marks

3. Look at these shapes.

   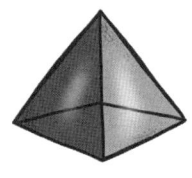 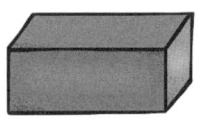 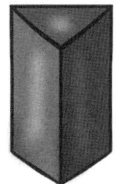  

   How many of them have at least one triangular face?

   .... shapes

   1 mark

4. Evie counted the animals she saw in a pond.

   She counted 9 newts. Add this to her tally chart.

Animal	Tally
Frog	||||	
Duck	||
Newt	

   1 mark

   How many animals did she count in total?

   .... animals

   1 mark

5. Finn adds 11 to a two-digit number.
   His new number has 8 tens and 5 ones.

   What number did he start with?

   ....

   2 marks

   END OF TEST

   / 8

Test 11

Warm up

1. Cross out the letters below that have a vertical line of symmetry.

   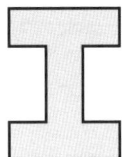 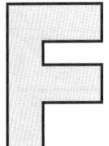  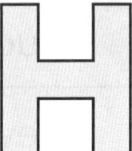

   1 mark

2. Find the missing number in each calculation.

   a) $70 + ? = 100$ ....

   b) $100 - ? = 10$ ....

   c) $? + 80 = 100$ ....

   2 marks

3. The flag on the right is divided into four equal parts.

   Fill in the missing numbers below.

   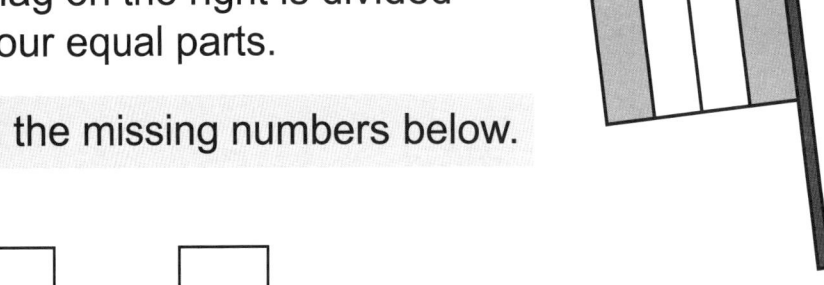

   1 mark

4. A hamster has 77 pellets in his food bowl.
He eats 13 pellets in the morning
and 9 pellets in the evening.

How many pellets are left in the bowl?

.... pellets

2 marks

5. Look at the clock on the right.

The **big hand** makes a
three-quarter turn clockwise.

What time is shown on the clock after the turn?

....

2 marks

END OF TEST

/ 8

Test 12

Warm up

1. Draw the next shape in this pattern.

   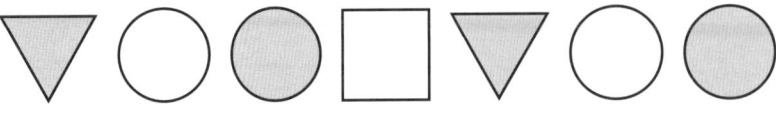 ....

   1 mark

2. Circle the **smallest** number in each list.

   a) thirty-three   thirteen   twenty-three

   b) eighty-seven   seventy-eight   eighty

   2 marks

3. The block diagram below shows how the pupils in Class 2A get to school.

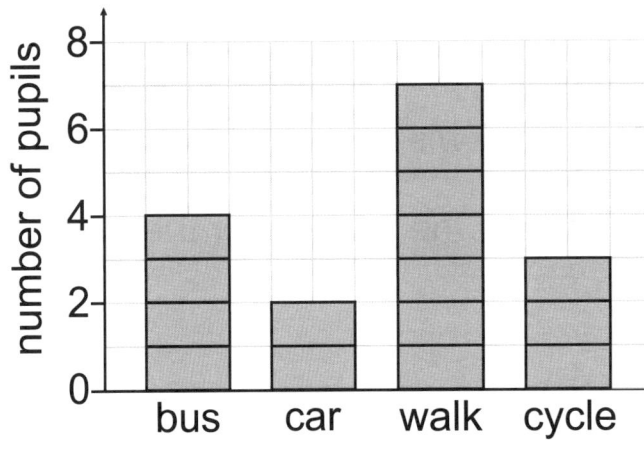

How many more pupils walk to school than cycle?

.... pupils

1 mark

4. Padma buys both of the snacks below.

She pays with **two 50p** coins.

How much change does she get?

 p

2 marks

5. Leon has four bags of 10 marbles.
He shares the marbles into five equal piles.

How many marbles are in each pile?

.... marbles

2 marks

END OF TEST

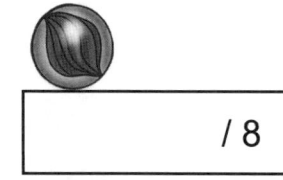

/ 8

Answers

Test 1 – pages 2-3

1. 6, 8, 10, 12, 14, 16 (**1 mark**)
2. a) 85 (**1 mark**)   b) 12 (**1 mark**)
3. E.g.

   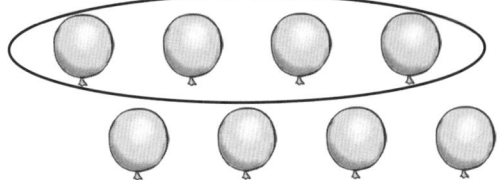

   (**1 mark for any four balloons circled**)
4. Amy (**1 mark**)
   Lydia (**1 mark**)
5. Any two of:
   1 + 7 = 8 (or 7 + 1 = 8)
   2 + 6 = 8 (or 6 + 2 = 8)
   3 + 5 = 8 (or 5 + 3 = 8)
   4 + 4 = 8

   (**1 mark for each correct sum, up to a total of two. Only award 1 mark if the same numbers have been used in each sum, e.g. 1 + 7 = 8 and 7 + 1 = 8.**)

Test 2 – pages 4-5

1. 9 – 7 = 2 and 7 – 5 = 2

   (**1 mark for each correct subtraction**)
2. 20 (**1 mark**)
3.

   9 kg (**1 mark**)

4.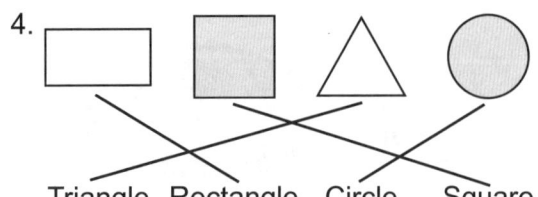

   (**2 marks for all four lines drawn correctly, otherwise 1 mark for two correct lines**)
5. 50p (**1 mark**)
   10p (**1 mark**)

Test 3 – pages 6-7

1. 11 + 9 and 14 + 6 should be circled.

   (**1 mark for each correct answer**)
2. a) Tuesday (**1 mark**)
   b) Saturday (**1 mark**)
3.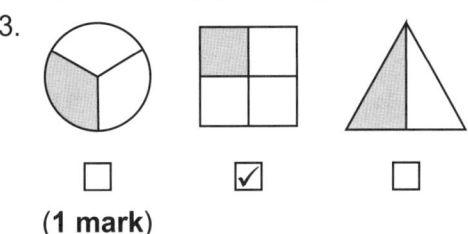

   (**1 mark**)
4. Jason (**1 mark**)
5. There are 2 × 3 = 6 bananas in two bunches. (**1 mark**)
   There are 4 × 3 = 12 bananas in four bunches. (**1 mark**)

Answers

Test 4 – pages 8-9

1. 1, 3, 5, 7, 9 (**1 mark**)

2. a) E.g.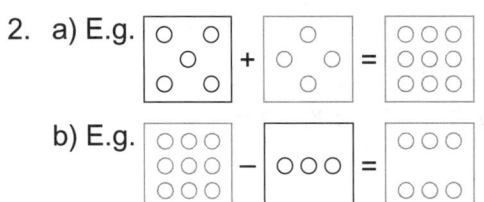
   b) E.g.

   (**1 mark for each correct answer**)

3.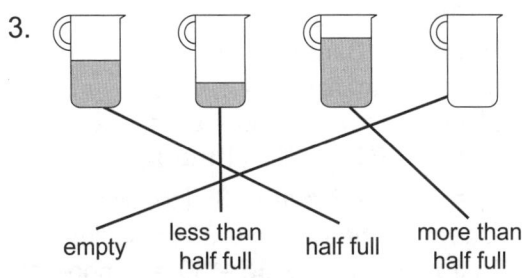

   (**2 marks for all four lines drawn correctly, otherwise 1 mark for two correct lines**)

4. The first and third shapes are cuboids. The second shape is a sphere. The fourth shape is a pyramid. So there are two cuboids. (**1 mark**)

5. A large rectangle represents a ten and a small rectangle represents a one, so 2 large rectangles and 8 small rectangles represents 20 + 8 = 28. 28 + 3 = 31, so Ben's number is 31, which is 3 large rectangles and 1 small rectangle:

   E.g.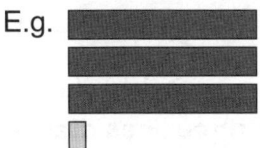

   (**2 marks for the correct number of large and small rectangles, otherwise 1 mark for any number of rectangles correctly showing 31**)

Test 5 – pages 10-11

1. 5 —one less→ 4 —five more→ 9

   (**1 mark for each correct number**)

2. 5 + 10 = 15, 15 − 5 = 10, 20 − 5 = 15, so 20 − 5 = 15 should be circled. (**1 mark**)

3. 'a quarter turn clockwise' should be circled. (**1 mark**)

   Ava makes a three-quarter turn clockwise. (**1 mark**)

4. 4 × 5 is the same as '4 lots of 5'. So 5 + 5 + 5 + 5 = 20 should be ticked. (**1 mark**)

5. 4 kg + 5 kg = 9 kg (**1 mark**)
   19 kg − 9 kg = 10 kg (**1 mark**)

Test 6 – pages 12-13

1. a) 16 (**1 mark**)   b) 10 (**1 mark**)

2. 1 + 4 + 5 = 10, so 1, 4 and 5 should be circled. (**1 mark**)

3. One **half** of shape A is shaded.
   Three **quarters** of shape B is shaded.

   (**1 mark for both correct**)

4. The lengths in order are:
   5 cm, 9 cm, 11 cm
   So the correct order of the bugs is:
   Spider, Worm, Slug (**1 mark**)

   length of the worm **<** length of the slug
   (**1 mark**)

5. The toys cost £2 + £5 = £7 in total. Subtract this from £10: £10 − £7 = £3. So she gets £3 change.

   (**2 marks for a correct answer, otherwise 1 mark for a correct method**)

Test 7 – pages 14-15

1. a) 8 × 2 (**1 mark**)   b) 5 × 5 (**1 mark**)
2. a) 37 (**1 mark**)   b) 84 (**1 mark**)
3.
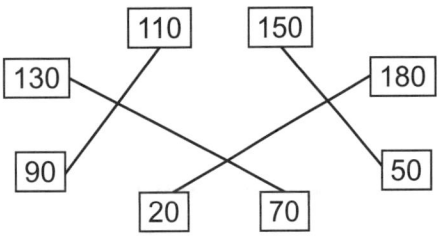

   (**2 marks for all four lines drawn correctly, otherwise 1 mark for two correct lines**)
4. The square has 4 sides, the hexagon has 6 sides and the triangle has 3 sides, so the order is:
   triangle, square, hexagon (**1 mark**)
5. Each small line on the scale is 1 cm, so the baby crocodile is 22 cm long. Partition 16 cm into 10 cm + 6 cm and add to 22 cm:
   22 cm + 10 cm = 32 cm,
   32 cm + 6 cm = 38 cm (**1 mark**)

Test 8 – pages 16-17

1. 16 (**1 mark**)
2. a) 14 (**1 mark**)   b) 20 (**1 mark**)
3.

   (**1 mark for each correct clock**)
4. C (**1 mark**)   A (**1 mark**)
5. Partition £15 into £10 + £5 and subtract from £27:
   £27 – £10 = £17, £17 – £5 = £12
   So £27 – £15 = £12 (**1 mark**)

Test 9 – pages 18-19

1. a) 99 (**1 mark**)   b) 43 (**1 mark**)
2. 2, 5, and 8 should be circled. (**1 mark**)
3. $\frac{1}{4}$ of 8 = 8 ÷ 4 = 2,
   so $\frac{3}{4}$ of 8 = 2 × 3 = 6
   (**1 mark**)
4. 1 hour = 60 minutes, so she runs for 60 + 2 = 62 minutes. (**1 mark**)
5. Partition £18 into £10 + £8 and subtract from £40:
   £40 – £10 = £30, £30 – £8 = £22
   So £40 – £18 = £22 (**1 mark**)
6. Masood has 3 × 10 = 30 ice lollies. Josephine has 7 × 5 = 35 ice lollies. So Josephine has 35 – 30 = 5 more ice lollies than Masood.
   (**2 marks for the correct answer, otherwise 1 mark for a correct method**)

Test 10 – pages 20-21

1.

   (**1 mark for both correct**)
2. 20 ÷ 5 (= 4) ——— 8 ÷ 2 (= 4)
   50 ÷ 10 (= 5)   6 ÷ 2 (= 3)
   15 ÷ 5 (= 3)   10 ÷ 2 (= 5)
   (**2 marks for all three lines drawn correctly, otherwise 1 mark for one correct line**)

3. 3 shapes have at least one triangular face (the first, third and fourth shapes). (**1 mark**)

4.
Animal	Tally
Frog	卌 I
Duck	II
Newt	卌 IIII

(**1 mark**)

She counted 6 frogs, 2 ducks and 9 newts. So she counted 6 + 2 + 9 = 17 animals in total. (**1 mark**)

5. His new number is 85. Subtract 11 to find the number he started with. Partition 11 into 10 + 1:
85 − 10 = 75, 75 − 1 = 74
So the number he started with was 74.

(**2 marks for the correct answer, otherwise 1 mark for a correct method**)

5. The big hand points to the 6. The small hand is between 9 and 10, so the time is half past nine. After a three-quarter turn clockwise, the big hand will point to the 3, and the small hand will have moved to just after the 10, so the time will be quarter past ten.

(**2 marks for the correct time, otherwise 1 mark for the correct hour**)

Test 11 – pages 22-23

1.

(**1 mark for both correct**)

2. a) 70 + **30** = 100
   b) 100 − **90** = 10
   c) **20** + 80 = 100

(**2 marks for all three correct, otherwise 1 mark for two correct**)

3. Two quarters are shaded, which is the same as one half, so:
$\frac{2}{4}$ or $\frac{1}{2}$ of the flag is shaded (**1 mark**)

4. He eats 13 + 9 = 22 pellets in total. Partition 22 into 20 + 2 and subtract from 77:
77 − 20 = 57, 57 − 2 = 55
So there are 55 pellets left in the bowl.

(**2 marks for the correct answer, otherwise 1 mark for a correct method**)

Test 12 – pages 24-25

1. ☐ (**1 mark**)

2. a) thirteen should be circled (**1 mark**)
   b) seventy-eight should be circled (**1 mark**)

3. 7 pupils walk to school and 3 pupils cycle to school. So 7 − 3 = 4 more pupils walk to school than cycle. (**1 mark**)

4. The snacks cost 40p + 35p = 75p. She pays 50p + 50p = 100p. So she gets 100p − 75p = 25p change.

(**2 marks for the correct answer, otherwise 1 mark for a correct method**)

5. He has 4 × 10 = 40 marbles in total. He shares 40 marbles into 5 equal piles, so there are 40 ÷ 5 = 8 marbles in each pile.

(**2 marks for the correct answer, otherwise 1 mark for a correct method**)

Progress Chart

That's all the tests in the book done — nice one!

Now fill in this table with all of your scores and see how you got on.

	Score
Test 1	
Test 2	
Test 3	
Test 4	
Test 5	
Test 6	
Test 7	
Test 8	
Test 9	
Test 10	
Test 11	
Test 12